SEW INTO SPORTS

Quilts for the Fans in Your Life

By Barbara Brackman

MINUTES
SECONDS
HOME
VISITOR
DOWN
TO GO
QTR

HOME OF THE
FLASHES

SEW INTO SPORTS

Quilts for the Fans in Your Life

By Barbara Brackman

Editor: Deb Rowden
Designer: Kelly Ludwig
Photography: Aaron T. Leimkuehler
Illustration: Eric Sears
Technical Editor: Kathe Dougherty
Production assistance: Jo Ann Groves

Published by:
Kansas City Star Books
1729 Grand Blvd.
Kansas City, Missouri, USA 64108

First edition, first printing
ISBN: 978-1-935362-48-7

Library of Congress Control Number: 2010927146
Printed in the United States of America by Walsworth Publishing Co., Marceline, MO

To order copies, call StarInfo at (816) 234-4636 and say "Books."

ABOUT THE AUTHOR

Barbara Brackman lives in Lawrence, Kansas, a sports town if ever there was one. It was, however, difficult to find photos of the author engaging in actual sports.

Barbara writes books inspired by antique quilts and designs reproduction fabrics for Moda/United Notions. Her most recent Star Books are *Juniper and Mistletoe* with Karla Menaugh and *The Carrie Hall Sampler*. She makes sports-themed quilts for her nieces and nephews.

ACKNOWLEDGEMENTS

Thanks to many friends who made quilts for the sports fans in their lives, and particularly to Jean Stanclift and Deb Rowden, both great collaborators. I am also grateful to the Library of Congress, which makes available so many great copyright-free pictures of our American past.

The author, age 12

Champion girls' basketball team, Chanute, Kansas, about 1911. Photo by J. M. Moore. From the collection of the Library of Congress.

CONTENTS

TEAM SPORTS

Over the last few years I've worked on several sports quilts for gifts, for charities and just for fun. The most important things I've discovered are:

THINK SPORTS!

and

THINK DEFENSE!

Think Sports

Many of the group quilts I've helped make were designed as fundraisers, quilts sold for charity. I've helped with intricate appliqués raffled to support the quilt guild, dog quilts for the Humane Society and house quilts auctioned for preservation projects. But the most money I've made for charity is with autographed sports quilts. Combining the interests of sports fans and quilt fans multiplies the audience. The pockets of sports enthusiasts tend to be deeper than those of quilt lovers.

Nascar Stars II by Mindy Peterson, 5acre Designs, Spring Hill, Kansas, 2001-2009. Quilted by Sandy Gore. 56" x 56".

Mindy collected signatures from Nascar drivers when she worked in the pits 10 years ago. The first Nascar Stars quilt was raffled to benefit the Ward Burton Wildlife Foundation. She saved a few blocks to make a small version for herself. The pattern is a traditional sawtooth star adapted for a friendship quilt by Possibilities.

Mindy Peterson's autographed Nascar Stars is a great example. She had a lot of fun getting the drivers' signatures at the races with the bonus thrill of signing a check for more than $5,000 to the charity.

Slam Dunk Shoe Quilt, see page 24.

Deb Rowden and I made a fundraising quilt signed by former basketball stars - those who played or coached at the University of Kansas. Opening the mailbox to find Dean Smith's and Roy William's autographs will make anybody's day, as will donating $2651 to buy school shoes for kids whose families can't afford to. Look for tips about collecting autographs from celebrities on pages 28-29.

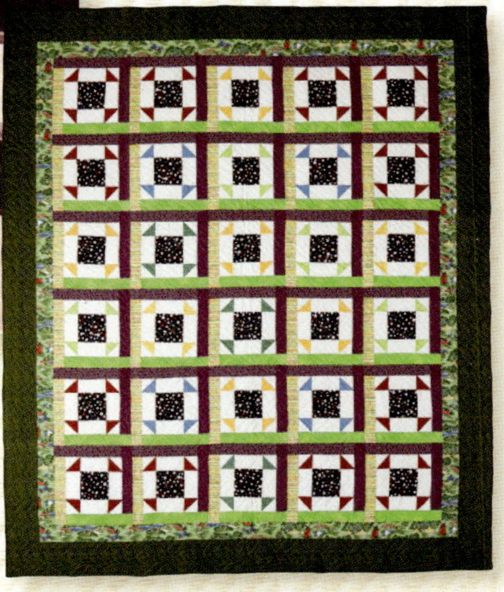

Hole in the Barn Door? No---Hole in One by Lavon Broyles Wynn. See page 55.

THINK SPORTS! for any kid's quilt. You can make beautiful florals and elaborate pieced quilts for your nieces and nephews, but don't actually present those gifts until the kids are 40. What they want now is a sports quilt. What you want is something simple that can be used and inevitably used up.

Detail of the Cody's Baseball Memory Quilt by Jean Pearson Stanclift. See page 34.

THINK SPORTS! as a memory quilt. Collecting signatures from teammates and friends in a high school baseball league will make a true keepsake quilt for a young relative.

Ty Cobb, 1912. Baseball cards from the Benjamin K. Edwards Collection at the Library of Congress. Ty Cobb was a terrific baseball player in the early 20th century, a famous example of an arrogant superstar. Think of your brash sports print as the Ty Cobb on your team and think defense!

Think Defense!

There are lots of sports fabrics out there - licensed prints for professional and college teams and generic pictorials featuring footballs, basketballs or hockey sticks. If you plan to use sports prints - THINK DEFENSE!

Sports fabrics are rarely team players. Whether they are licensed logos or baseball pictorials, they tend to be bright, brash and full of clashing primaries. We can compare a sports print to a sports star - an arrogant super-athlete. Put one of those larger-than-life prints in your quilt and it will take over. Put a lot of them in your quilt and you've got a fight on your hands. If you aren't a careful manager, your quilt could wind up the visual equivalent of a hockey melee.

A primary problem is the primary colors. Garish team colors work great for keeping track of players from the bleacher seats. They create a player image and a fan identity, but they can limit the look of the quilt.

Designers who create generic sports fabric like to throw in the primaries (red, blue and yellow) with a lot of grass green and shades of brown for the balls and the bats. Go with that palette and you have bright colors accented with pigskin brown, a color scheme you wouldn't have picked if you were managing the team.

St. Louis, late 1950s. The Thilking sisters, Gloria and Marilyn, are ready to take on the Williams sisters or any other doubles partners.

THINK DEFENSE

You are managing the team!

What you need to do is control that superstar, the sports print. Let it play - you need it. But complement the center of attention with a team of your own choice. Build a squad of reliable backup players with their own identities. We've used a lot of bright colors to redirect the quilt's palette. If the team colors are fire engine red and cobalt blue, use a team of softer yellows to shift the play your way. If the print features unpleasant group dynamics ignore those colors and push the whole design to black and white, lime green or pink. (Yes, pink!)

We've also signed up a lot of strong pattern. Dots, stripes and checks have individual personalities that become stars on their own. And don't forget the officials - umpires and referees in black and white stripes. The biggest bully on the team will settle down with a border of black and white checks.

ASSEMBLE A TEAM TO BACK UP YOUR SPORTS PRINTS

Prints & Pattern

- Spots
- Checks
- Stripes
- Stars
- Prints that read as solids from any distance
- Batiks
- Tone on tone

Colors

- Red, blue and yellow are the primaries - the colors most teams choose for official colors. Many generic sports prints feature a true grassy green. Push the play your way by trying some of these.
- Lime green
- Pink and magenta
- Black as the background
- Toned-down shades of the team colors—for example, grayed blues or navy make a bright blue pop. Wheat straw yellows and steel grays are great defense against a tiger yellow and black palette.
- Add a range of color. If the team color is red, assemble 12 different reds as back-up—brick to wine red.

PROJECT 1

OUT OF BOUNDS

Out of Bounds, pieced and designed by Barbara Brackman, quilted by Lori Kukuk, 2010, Lawrence, Kansas, 55 1/2" x 70".

My grandniece Kayla is a big San Diego Padres fan and an even bigger fan of pink. The soccer quilt is for her big-girl bed.

Girls love pink and girls love soccer. Here a black and white soccer print teams up with spots, checks and stripes. It's a natural combination in the supernatural pinks so popular today for female fashion.

A Housetop quilt, collection of Deb Rowden.

I love this log cabin variation known as "housetops" among the quilters of Gees Bend, Alabama, whose colorful quilts have popularized a design with 19th-century roots. The simple square-inside-a-square-inside-a-square lets you focus on color, contrast and print because there's minimal measuring and planning. Cut squares and strips and sew. It all works out in the end - especially if you have a 15" square plastic ruler and a new blade in your rotary cutter.

Middy blouses and bloomers were standard uniforms for these soccer players about 1920. From the collection of the Library of Congress.

Fabric Requirements

Blocks

- Sports print for centers: 1/2 yard
- 1/3 yard of 4 pinks (you'll have extra pinks from the border fabric too)
- 1/3 yard of 6 black & white dots, checks and stripes (buy an extra 1/2 yard of 1 stripe for the binding)

Borders

Note: Cut the borders first and use the extra pink yardage in the blocks.

- Dark pink for inner border piece: 1 3/4 yards
- Wide black and white stripe for middle border: 1/2 yard (cut across the stripes)

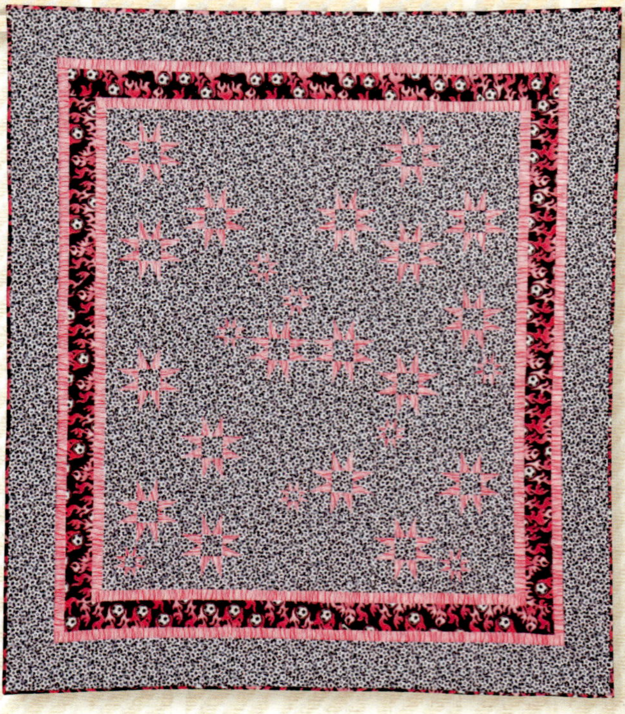

Soccer Fever, made for Kate Liston by Denniele Bohannon, Harrisonville, Missouri, 2009. Quilted by Louise Lewis. 63" x 63".

- Light pink for outer border: 2 yards
- Backing: 3 1/2 yards
- Binding: 1/2 yard

Optional

- A plastic ruler 15" square to square up the blocks

Cutting

Blocks

- From the sports print, cut 12 squares 6" x 6".
- From the pinks, cut strips 3" x the width of the fabric (wof), about 42".
- From the black & white prints, cut strips 2 1/2" x wof.

Borders

Inner border

- Cut from dark pink fabric: 2 strips 2" x 47" for top and bottom borders.
- Cut 2 strips 2" x 58 1/2" for side borders.

Middle border

- Cut across the striped fabric: 4 strips 2" x wof for top and bottom borders. (Piece these together to make 2 strips 2" x 50".)
- Cut 4 strips 2" x wof for side borders. (Piece these together to make 2 strips 2" x 62 1/2".)

Outer border

- Cut from light pink fabric: 2 strips 3 1/2" x 56" for top and bottom borders.
- Cut 2 strips 3 1/2" x 65 1/2" for side borders.

Soccer team about 1920. Women athletes were hampered by attitudes about their abilities and by the clothing that society required they wear. From the collection of the Library of Congress.

SEW-AND-TRIM LOG CABIN BLOCKS

About 1890 a pattern company known as the Ladies' Art Company published this design of concentric dark and light squares under the name White House Steps. I interviewed a woman in Washington state several years ago who told me her mother made this design for all the boys in the family. The girls received Sunbonnet Sue quilts. (We can hope times have changed.)

This sew-and-trim method for Log Cabin blocks relies on a cutter, small ruler and small cutting mat kept close to your machine. A 15" square ruler also makes this easy and fast when you do the final trim.

Work on 2 blocks at a time so you never have to snip the thread until you're finished with all the blocks.

Block Assembly

1. Begin with a center square A.
2. Trim the selvages off the ends of a 3" pink strip and cut the wof strip in half so you have 2 strips, each about 20" long. This will be your first round of logs (B & C).
3. Stitch one strip to the top and one to the bottom of the square.
4. Trim the strips so you have a rectangle BAB.
5. Using the leftover strips, stitch one strip to either side of that rectangle.
6. Trim the strips so you have a square with piece C on either side. Press.
7. Cut 2 matching 2 1/2" black and white strips for your second round of logs (D & E) into 2 strips each, one about 12" long, the other about 28".
8. Stitch one shorter strip to the top and one shorter strip to the bottom of the square.
9. Trim the strips so you have a rectangle with Ds on either side.
10. Stitch one of the longer strips to either side of that rectangle.
11. Trim the strips so you have a square with a piece E on either side. Press.
12. You can continue going like on like this, adding strips and trimming to make ever larger concentric squares, but for the Out of Bounds quilt, stop here.
13. Repeat to make 12 blocks.
14. Check blocks to make sure each is 15" square.

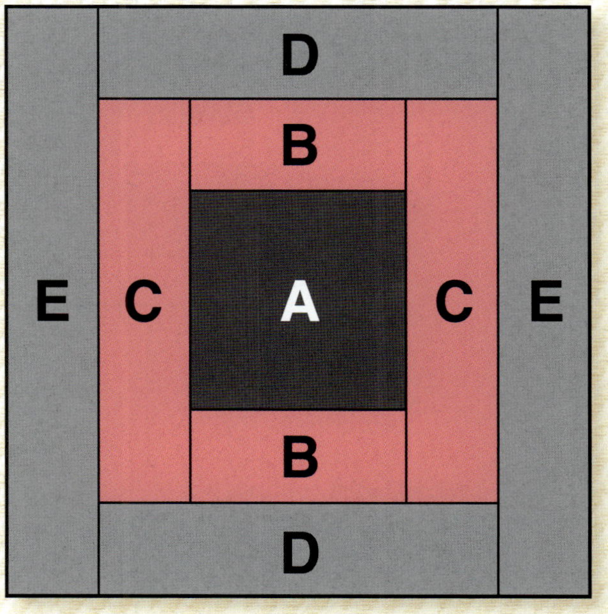

Block

Assembly Diagram

Quilt Assembly

- Stitch 4 rows of 3 blocks each.
- Stitch the rows together.
- Add the side inner borders of dark pink, then the top and bottom borders.
- Add the black and white middle borders (2" x 62 1/2") to the sides. Then add the top and bottom (2" x 50") borders.
- Add the side outer borders of light pink, then the top and bottom borders.

Quilting

Lori Kukuk designed the machine quilting featuring soccer balls in the center squares and meandering squiggles in the border and blocks. See the quilting pattern on page 52.

PROJECT 2

SPIKE

***Spike* by Barbara Brackman, quilted by Lori Kukuk, 2009, Lawrence, Kansas, 37 1/2" x 37 1/2".**

Volleyball provided some entertainment for young Japanese Americans imprisoned at California's Manzanar Internment Camp during World War II. Photo by Ansel Adams from the Library of Congress, 1943.

Sydnei Patton, 2008. Her neighbor Lavon Wynn made a quilt recalling Sydnei's love of ballet and sports. See it on page 54.

Sports prints tend to come in red, blue, yellow, green plus the color of the ball. That may be too many colors. This volleyball quilt spikes up the palette by going for the true primaries, red, blue and yellow, and echoing the white ball. Stripes and dots add to the energy. The Log Cabin blocks are pieced straight and then trimmed on a slant to make what people are calling Wonky Log Cabins.

Fabric Requirements

- 1 1/2 yards of sports print for blocks and backing
- For the logs: 1 regular quarter yard of each of the following:
- 3 reds
- 3 blues
- 2 yellows (buy an extra 1/2 yard of one for the binding)
- 1 white

Border

- 1/4 yard of a black and white stripe

Optional

- A plastic ruler 15" square to square up the blocks

Cutting

Blocks

- From the sports print: cut 9 squares 5 1/2" x 5 1/2" for the block centers.
- From the other fabrics: cut strips of varying sizes across the width of fabric (wof).
- Cut strips from 1 1/2" to 3 1/2" wide x wof.

Border

- Cut from striped fabric: 2 strips 2" x 35" for side borders. Cut across the stripes.
- Cut 2 strips 2" x 38" for top and bottom borders.

Block Assembly

Refer to the block assembly instructions for Sew-and-Trim Log Cabin blocks on page 13. Follow steps 1 to 12. The major difference here is smaller center squares and strips of varying sizes.

Build up the logs until you have a square that is at least 13" x 13". Some blocks had 2 strips, some 3 to achieve that size. The larger the square, the wonkier your final cut can be.

New step 14: trim your blocks to 12" but turn the ruler so the center square and logs are at an angle.

You need 9 - 12" square blocks.

Quilt Assembly

- Stitch 3 rows of 3 blocks each.
- Stitch the rows together.
- Add the side borders, then the top and bottom borders resulting in a top measuring 38" x 38".

Quilting

Lori Kukuk machine quilted a sunburst over every other block and a meandering line in the rest.

Assembly Diagram

PROJECT 3

PIECED PIGSKIN

Pieced Pigskin, by Deb Gehlbach Rowden. Quilted by Lori Kukuk, 2009, Lawrence, Kansas, 25" x 25". Collection of Walt Gehlbach.

Deb pieced a football quilt for her dad who played offensive and defensive tackle at Kansas State University in 1948-50. On the back, she framed a fabric collage combining an old program with a photo of Walt in action.

A pieced football can be appliquéd to a background or pieced into it. We give you instructions for both methods. Use striped or checked fabric to indicate the laces and ask friends and teammates to autograph the stripes.

A candid sports shot of the author about 1950, holding a football for her wary brother, Bill.

Fabric Requirements

Note: fat quarters measure 18" x 22".

Note: All the fabrics are brown ranging from light tan to dark brown. Cut the block pieces first and use extra for the strip-pieced border.

- 1 fat quarter of striped or checked fabric for the laces
- Block backgrounds: 4 fat quarters in tan geometrics (or 1/2 yard if you want it to be all the same for signature space)
- 1 fat quarter of light or white for the stripes on the ball
- Footballs – 4 fat quarters in dark browns
- Borders: If you'd prefer a single piece of sports-themed fabric for the border, buy 1 yard. For the piano-key strip border shown, you'll have enough with leftovers from the blocks.
- Backing: 1 yard
- Binding: 1/2 yard

Cutting

Blocks

Note: add seam allowances to all pattern pieces.

- Using the templates on page 21: cut the pieces as indicated. Repeat 4 times.
- If you intend to appliqué the pieced football to a background, do not cut piece A for the backgrounds. Instead cut 4 squares from the tan geometrics 9 1/2" x 9 1/2".
- For a scrappy background: cut 8 strips of various light fabrics into rectangles 9 1/2" x 5" to piece together in pairs for background squares.

Border

For the strip-pieced border: cut your remaining fabrics into strips ranging in width from 1 1/2" to 2 1/2" wide. Stitch these together and trim to get the following border strips:

- Cut 2 strips 4" x 18 1/2" for the side borders.
- Cut 2 strips 4" x 25 1/2" for the top and bottom borders.

Block Assembly

- Piece a D unit to either side of the laces (E).
- Add a C unit to either end and then a B to create the football.
- If you are piecing the block, add an A unit to either side of the football.
- If you are appliquéing the football to a background, glue or baste the edges of the football under. Stitch using your favorite appliqué method.

Paper piecing works well for this block. Follow the numbers on the pattern on page 21.

Two generations of cheerleaders. My sister Jane (back row, third from left), about 1964, and her stepdaughter Natasha Holcomb about 1992.

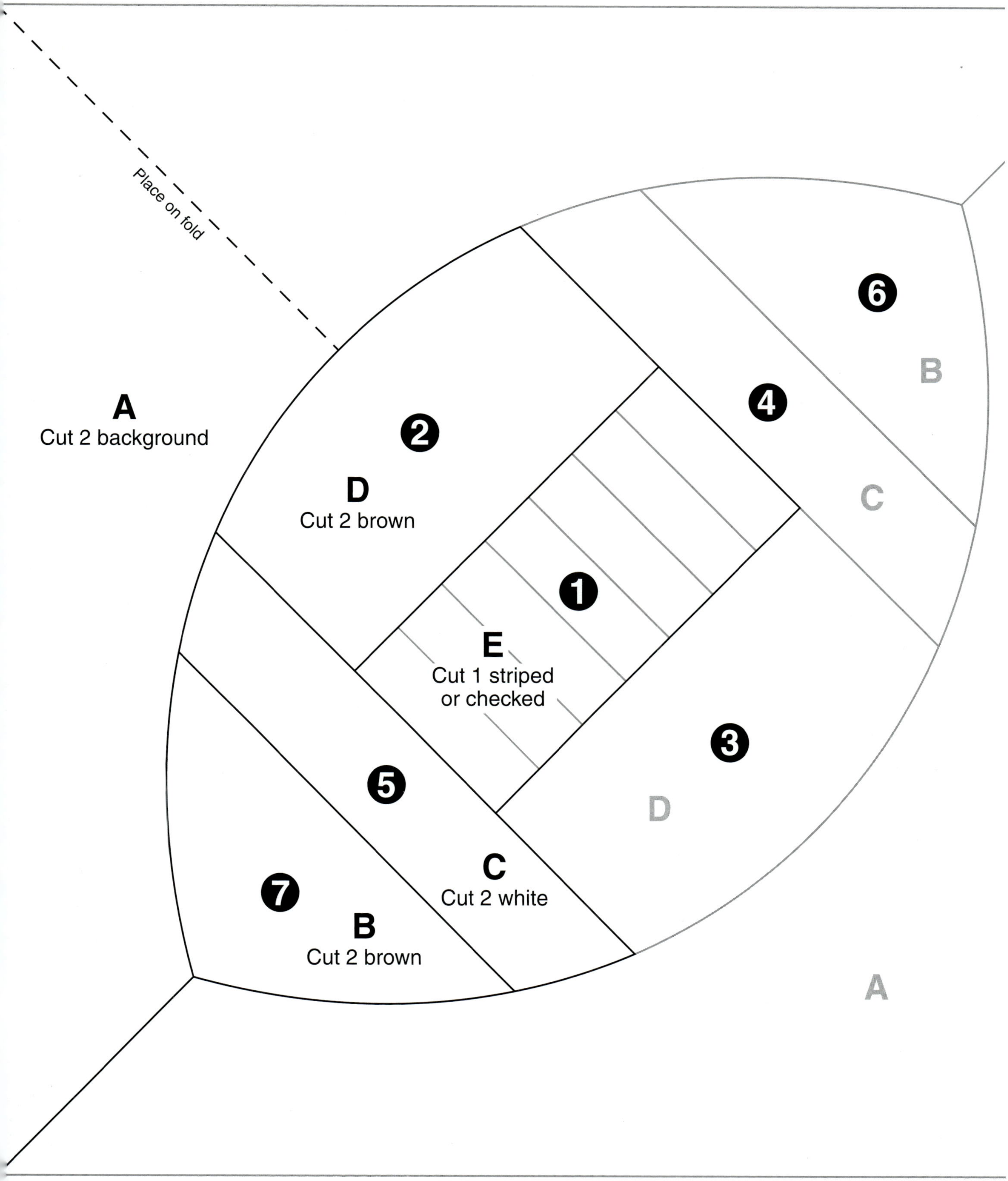

1 thru 7 paper piecing order.

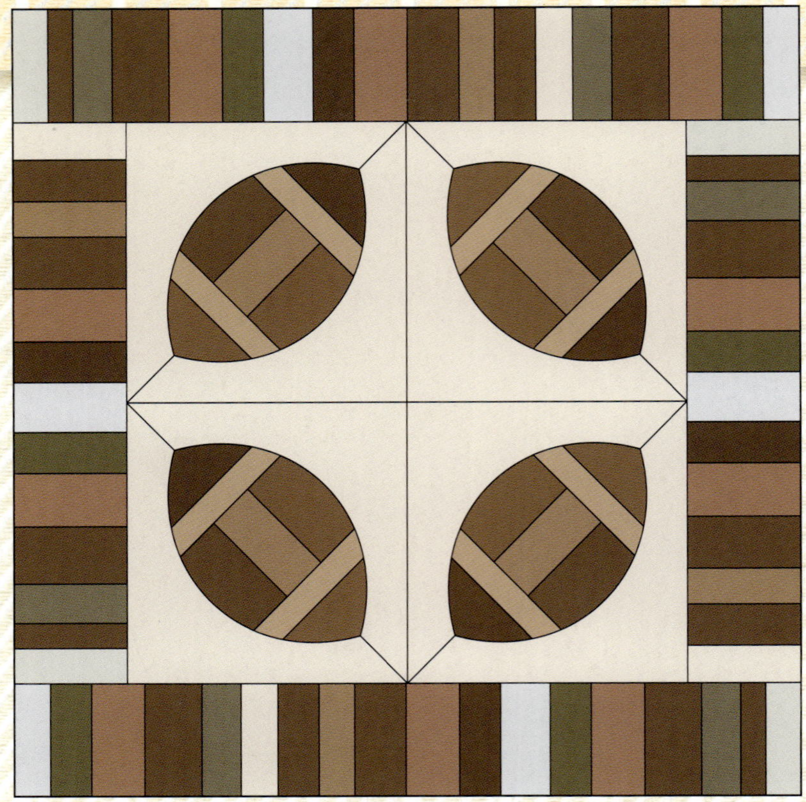

Assembly Diagram

Quilt Assembly

- Arrange the blocks in 4 different directions as shown.
- Stitch 2 pairs of 2 blocks. Join these strips.
- Add the side borders, then add the top and bottom borders.

Quilting

Lori Kukuk machine quilted a kind of flourish outside the balls and did some echo quilting in the center. She created a string of footballs in the border.

Cody's Football Memory Quilt by Jean Stanclift. Quilted by Lori Kukuk, 2010, Lawrence, Kansas, 42" x 42".

Jean pieced the football and then appliquéd it to a white background square (10" finished) so she'd have extra room for the names of Cody's teammates in junior high football. She alternated log cabin blocks framing photo-transferred portraits of him in seventh, eighth and ninth grades. His award letter is loosely attached to the block at the bottom left, so he can remove it if he wants to put it on a letter jacket. Lori quilted a string of footballs in the 4" blue border. The outer border is pieced of 2" finished sawtooth squares.

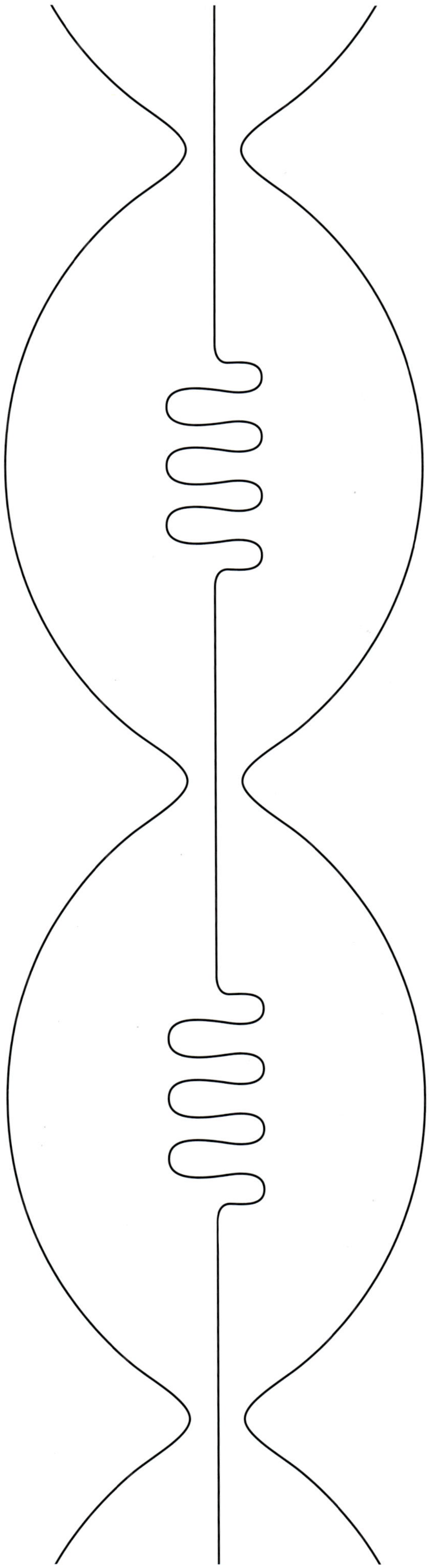

Border quilting pattern

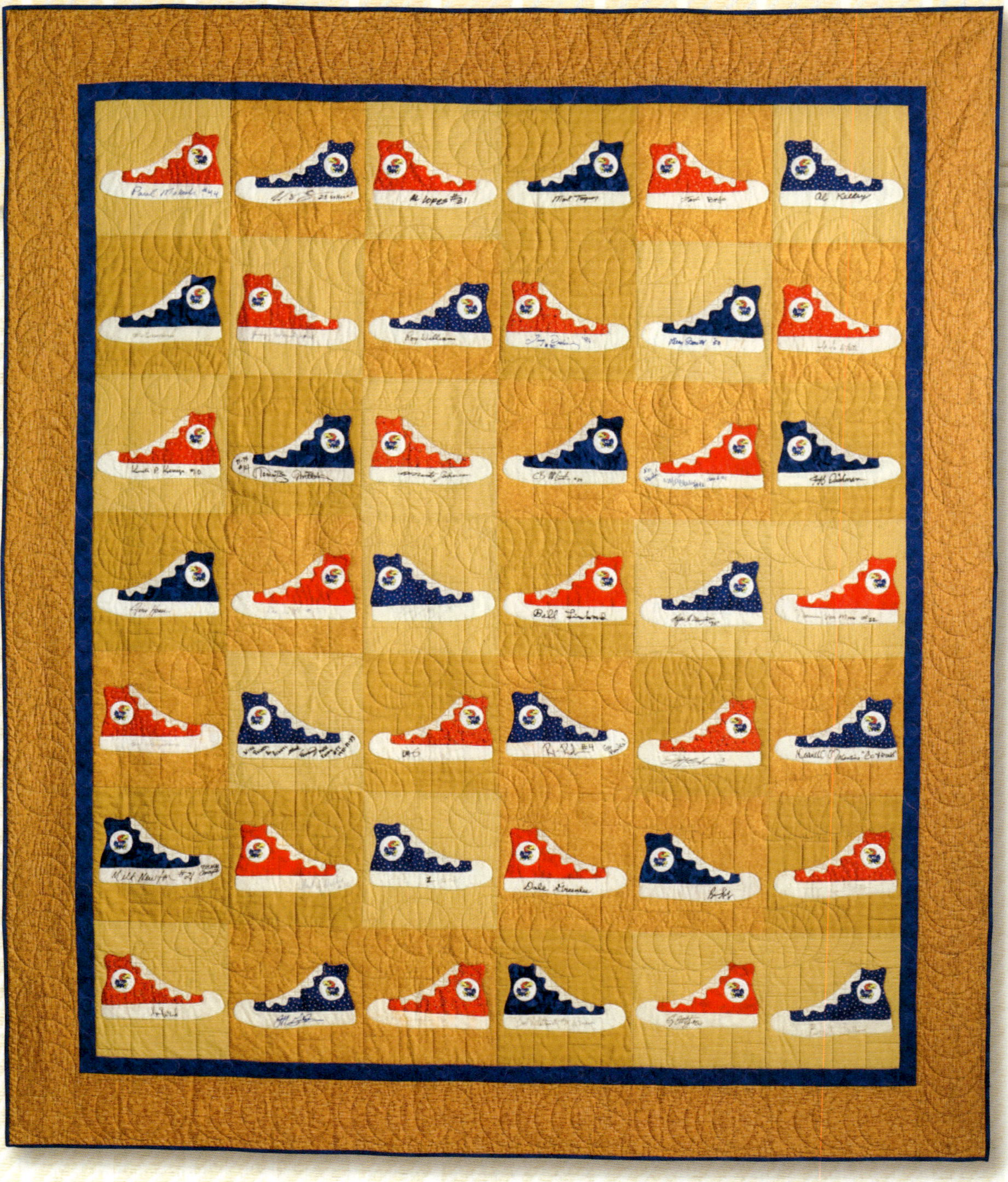

PROJECT 4

SLAM DUNK SHOE QUILT

***Slam Dunk Shoe Quilt*, by Jean Stanclift and Deb Rowden. Designed by Deb Rowden and Barbara Brackman, quilted by Rosie Mayhew, 2006, Lawrence, Kansas, 87" x 99".**

Kelvin Clark makes an impossible shot in 1986. *See the quilt his mother made on page 56.*

Basketball at Western High School in Washington, DC, 1899. Photo by Frances Benjamin Johnston, from the Library of Congress.

A label on the back of the quilt lists the block signatures.

Gloria E. Clark played for the Stallions at FL Schlagle High School in Kansas City, Kansas in 1989. *See the quilt her mother made to recall the family's superstars on page 56.*

The basketball memory quilt was a team project to raise money for a local school shoe fund. Deb Rowden and her daughter Kate gathered signatures of former Kansas University stars who played or coached from the 1940s through 2005.

Kate interviewed friends and fans to generate a list of their favorite alums. She and her Uncle Gregg Gehlbach found many addresses on the internet and contacted 60 athletes. Friends who were lucky enough to know a player collected signatures at the dentist's office or a neighborhood hangout.

Barbara Brackman drew the pattern, Deb Rowden picked the fabrics and assembled blocks appliquéd by Jean Stanclift. Rosie Mayhew quilted it on her longarm machine.

Jayhawker, by Thelma E. Humphrey, 1934-1935, who collected autographs from members of the Athletic Department at the University of Kansas while a KU student. Decades later while living in Ottawa she finished the quilt by embroidering the signatures. The quilting was done by her mother, Annettia.

My sister Jane was a basketball coach at Blue Valley High School near Kansas City in the 1970s.

Fabric Requirements

Block

- Circle (piece A): 1 yard sports team logo or star print to fussy cut
- Shoes (piece C): 4 pieces 3/4 yard each in team colors to mix and match
- Soles & Laces (pieces B & D): 1 1/2 yards white (if you are sending soles off to celebrities you may want to buy more because some will not return. See pages 28-29 for tips on gathering signatures.)
- Block backgrounds: 4 pieces 1 1/2 yards each in prints the color of a hardwood floor

Borders

- Inner border and binding: 1 1/2 yard team color
- Outer border: 3 yards hardwood floor color
- Backing: 8 yards

Cutting

Blocks

- Cut 42 pieces of background fabric into 12 1/2" squares.
- Cut templates from pieces A-D, adding seam allowances.
- For each shoe, cut 1 A-D as described on templates.
- We reversed about half the shoes for a balanced look.

Borders

- Inner border: Cut 8 - 2" strips. Piece together to make 2 - 75 1/2" strips for the top and bottom borders. Save the leftover lengths. To make side strips, piece 2 – 2" strips with 1 leftover strip (if needed) for each side. Trim each to 84 1/2".
- Outer border: Cut 4 strips 6 1/2" x 87 1/2".

Block Assembly

- Gather signatures on the soles (piece D).
- Appliqué the shoes using your favorite method. Jean machine-appliquéd over freezer paper and removed the freezer paper when the blocks were finished.
- Appliqué A and B to C before positioning C on the background.
- Stitch down the shoe and add the sole D last.

Quilt Assembly

- Arrange the blocks for a balanced look of left and right shoes.
- Stitch 7 rows of 6 blocks each.
- Attach the rows.
- Add the side inner borders, then the top and bottom borders.
- Add the side outer borders, then the top and bottom borders.

Quilting

Rosie Mayhew designed the machine quilting featuring bouncing basketballs in the borders and in the open areas between the shoes. See the basketball quilting pattern on page 51.

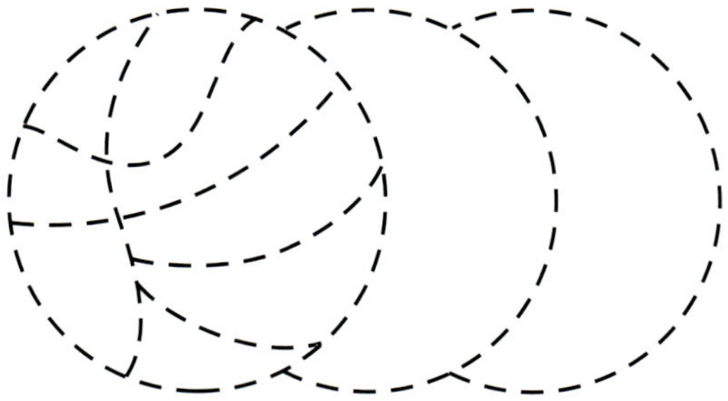

Bouncing ball quilting design

Forrest C. "Phog" Allen's signature on the Jayhawk quilt.

Tips for Gathering Signatures

Signatures on Nascar Stars II by Mindy Peterson, 5acre Designs.

Detail of Slam Dunk Shoe Quilt, see page 24. Dean Smith lettered at Topeka High School and the University of Kansas in the early 1950s. He coached the basketball team at the University of North Carolina for 36 years.

You're smart to gather signatures on a fabric swatch rather than on a finished block in case of errors, blotches or unreturned mail. For the shoe autographs, we cut shoe soles and ironed them to freezer paper templates to stabilize them for writing. For the footballs, you might ask players to sign a white stripe; for the bowling quilt, have teammates sign the balls before you appliqué the holes.

Gathering signatures in person

- Cut and mount a lot of shoe soles, football stripes or plain fabric.
- Always carry along a permanent marker or two.
- Take them to your kid's practice, games and meetings.
- If you feel like you are being a pest waiting for signatures, hand teammates a packet with fabric, explanation and a self-addressed, stamped envelope. Ask them to sign in pencil and you'll go over it later with a permanent marker.

Gathering signatures by mail

Celebrities are surprisingly generous with their signatures, especially if you make it clear you are raising money for a charity.

There are problems with student athletes, however, because they often aren't permitted to sign anything that raises money–even for a good cause. That's why we asked former college athletes to sign our basketball quilt.

You need a street address. We found lots on the internet. Good prospects are athletes who've gone on to play on professional teams. Look up the pro-teams. Address the player in care of the team.
Again, *don't send the whole block*. You may never see it again.
We mailed each athlete a shoe sole with an explanation sheet, a permission sheet, and a self-addressed stamped envelope. See sample forms below.
Include a flier about the charity.

A note about permanent markers

The most archival markers (those that are going to last the longest) are Pigma pens. Laundry markers like Sharpies fade over time.

Sample Explanation Sheet for Autographs for Charity

We're making a quilt to raise money for {charity}. We'd love to have your autograph on one of the blocks. Can you help us out by signing the piece of fabric we've enclosed? We'll sew your signature into the quilt.

Please sign the piece on the fabric side, not the paper side. Use a laundry maker or other permanent felt tip pen. If you haven't got one, sign in pencil and we'll trace the pencil line to make it permanent.

Sign the permission form too, please. Give us an address and we'll let you know how the project goes.

Mail the fabric and permission form back in the self-addressed stamped envelope. We'd like the signed fabric back by {date}.

Thanks! {include your name, email and the street address}

Sample Permission Form

I hereby give {your name} permission to use my autograph in a fundraising quilt to raise money for {charity} and to use my name in publicity related to the quilt and its sale.

Signed

Date

Cody Stanclift, 2009

My sister Jane's high school scrapbook includes photos of the student/faculty basketball game at Shawnee Mission East in the 1960s. She likens the battle-hardened soldiers to the defense they bested at the annual female football game.

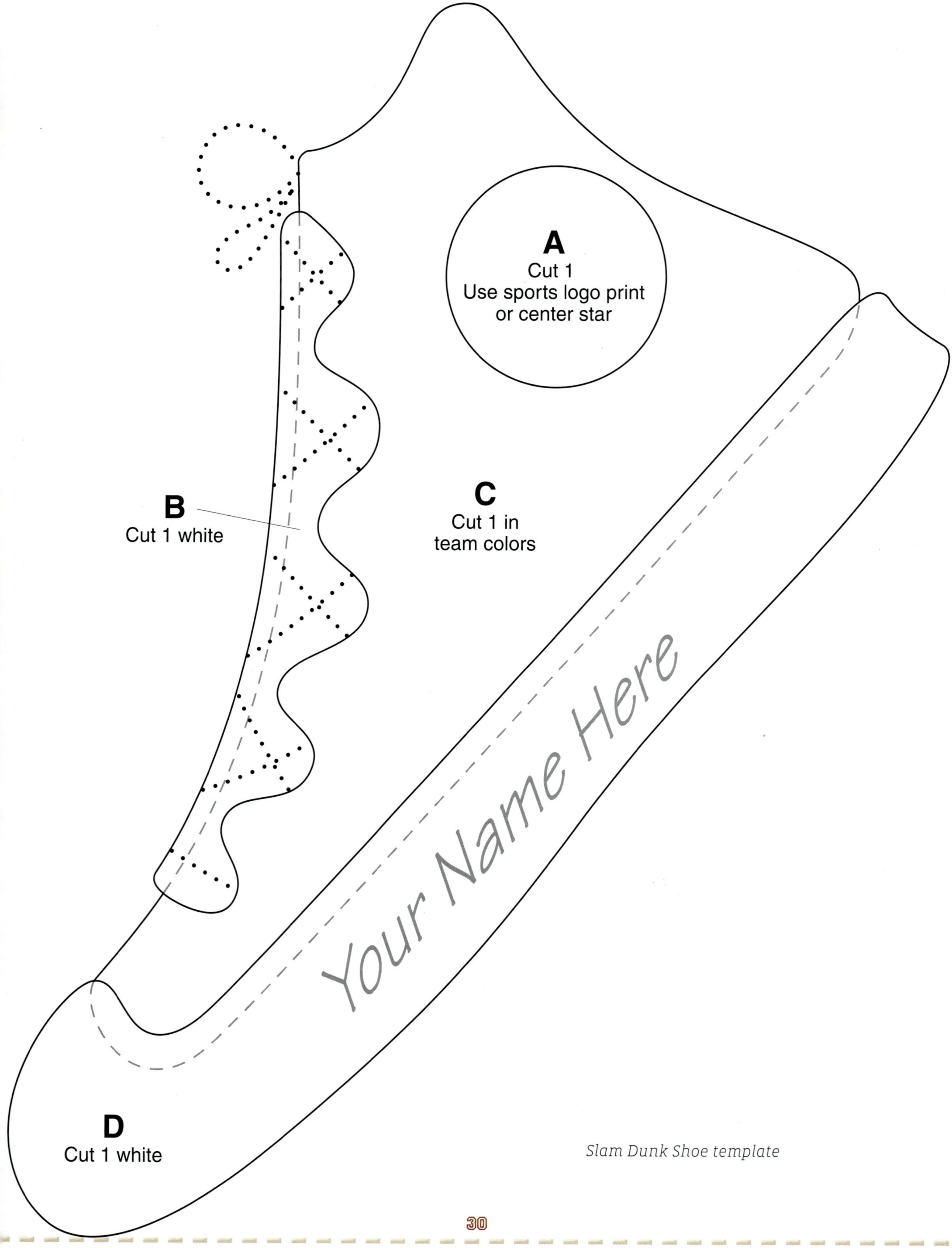

Slam Dunk Shoe template

PROJECT 5

SNOW GLOBE

Snow Globe by Barbara Brackman, Lawrence, Kansas, 2008. 23" x 23".

Sarah Rucker as a freshman in the KU Band, 2009.

Detail of Jayhawker autograph quilt (see pages 3 and 26) with James Naismith's signature. Born in Canada in 1861, Naismith was coaching at the YMCA in Springfield, Massachusetts when he came up with the game of basketball. He brought the game to Kansas in 1899.

I made my first Snow Globe quilt as a wedding present for a snow globe collector, highlighting pictorial prints with a simple appliquéd circle and base. Your sports fan will love a snow globe wall hanging featuring the team mascot. Frame sports equipment, a catcher's glove or a ballet shoe. Go with team colors or create a winter wonderland with a starry blue sky behind the circles. This appliqué is so simple it makes a good beginner's project.

Fabric Requirements

Blocks

Note: fat quarters measure 18" x 22".

- Globe (A) Team pictorial print. You need enough yardage for 9 logos. A half yard should be enough but check to make sure you have 9 repeats.
- Base (B) 1 fat quarter dark
- Backgrounds: I mixed blues from 4 fat quarters, but 1/2 yard will give you enough for 9 identical backgrounds and binding.

Borders

- Sashing and borders: 1/2 yard
- Backing: 3/4 yard
- Binding: 1/4 yard of background color

Cutting

Blocks

- Background: Cut 9 squares 5 1/2" x 5 1/2".
- Snow globes: Using the templates on page 33 cut as directed adding a seam allowance.
- For circle A: center your pictorial figure.

Sashing and border

- For the top and bottom borders: cut 2 strips 2 1/2" x 23 1/2"

- For the vertical strips between the blocks: cut 4 strips 2 1/2" x 19 1/2"
- For the horizontal strips: cut 6 rectangles 2 1/2" x 5 1/2"

Assembly diagram

Block Assembly

- Prepare the snow globes (A) by basting or gluing the edges under.
- For the base (B) it is only necessary to turn the side edges under. Leave the top and bottom as raw edges. Baste or glue the side edges.
- Center the circles with about 1" around the top and sides.
- Place the base under the circle with the bottom edge overlapping the edge of the background.
- Baste or glue in place.
- Appliqué using your favorite method.

Quilt Assembly

- Stitch a horizontal strip to the bottom of one block.
- Repeat to make a vertical column of 3 blocks with sashing between them.
- Repeat to make 3 columns. Press.
- Stitch a vertical strip between 2 columns.
- Add another vertical strip and the last column to make the field.
- Add a vertical column on either side.
- Finish by adding the top and bottom borders. Press.

Quilting

Barbara hand quilted by echoing the circles and the blocks inside and out.

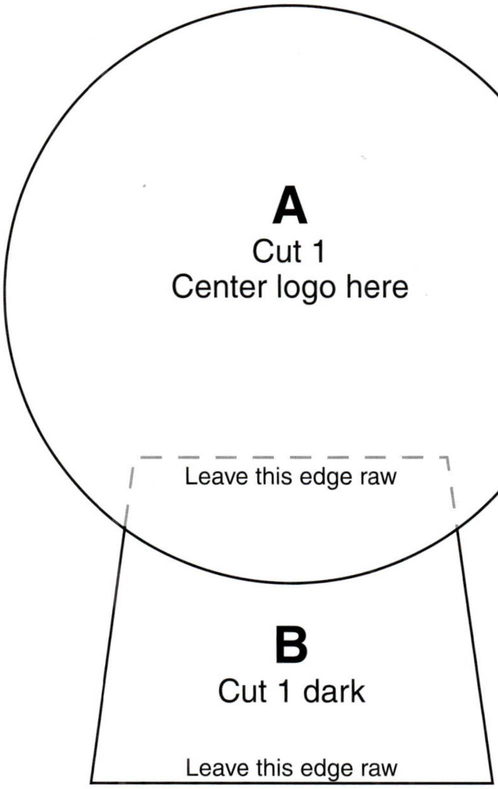

PROJECT 6

CODY'S BASEBALL MEMORY

***Cody's Baseball Memory* by Jean Stanclift, quilted by Lori Kukuk, 2008, Lawrence, Kansas, 65" x 77". Collection of Cody Stanclift.**

The Yankees outfield in 1915. Collection of the Library of Congress.

After making the Slam Dunk Shoe Quilt, Jean and Barbara realized they could design a baseball memory quilt for Jean's son Cody, an all-round athlete in grade school and junior high.

Barbara drew the block and Jean designed a quilt in Cody's Kansas Rebels team colors, using his uniform for two blocks. She gathered signatures on the shoe soles from his coaches and teammates (see pages 28-29 for Tips on Gathering Signatures.) The shoes also could be appliquéd for a football, soccer or field hockey team as the styles are similar. For more sports shoes patterns, see page 48.

Cody's team colors could have been brighter but Jean toned down the palette by graying the whites and darkening the reds.

Cody Stanclift started playing baseball when he was 6. He was invited to join a traveling team, the Kansas Rebels, in third grade and played shortstop for them till he was 12.

Fabric Requirements

Jean cut up Cody's baseball uniform shirt, using the front and the back for blocks so she needed only 18 shoes. The cutting and yardage here give you enough for 20 shoe blocks.

Blocks

- Block backgrounds: 4 pieces 1 1/2 yards each in team colors
- Shoes (pieces A & C): 4 pieces 3/4 yard each in team colors to mix and match
- Soles & Laces (pieces B & D): 1 1/2 yards gray or other light color

Borders

- Sawtooth border: You can probably get all the fabric you need from leftovers from the background and shoe fabrics, but if you want a different colored border buy 1/2 yard each of 2 contrasting colors.
- Middle strip: same gray as shoe soles and laces – see above. (Cut the border before the soles and laces.)
- Outer border: 2 yards dark
- Backing: 4 yards sports print
- Binding: 1/2 yard

Cutting

Blocks/Backgrounds

Note: If you are using a tshirt or uniform, center the images and words and cut 12 1/2" squares.

- Cut 10 red and 10 black 12 1/2" squares.

Appliquéd Shoes

- Add seams to appliqué pieces A-D and cut from the templates on page 37.
- For each shoe, cut 1 A-D as described on templates.
- Note: Jean reversed about half the shoes for a balanced look.

Borders

Sawtooth border (finishing to 2" wide)

You may have your own method for creating sawtooth blocks. We'll give you the basics here.

- Cut 56 red squares and 56 black 2 7/8" squares.
- Cut each of these diagonally into 2 triangles.
- You need 112 triangles of each color.

Middle strip border

- Cut 2 strips 1" x 63 1/2" for the side borders.
- Cut 2 strips 1" x 52 1/2"for the top and bottom borders.

Outer Border

- Cut 4 strips 6 1/2" x 64 1/2".

Sarah Stanclift

Athletics have been an important family activity for the Stanclifts. Cody's older brother Michael and sister Sarah played baseball too. Jean gets a lot of handwork done at games.

Block Assembly

- Gather signatures on the soles (piece D).
- Appliqué the shoes using your favorite method. Jean machine-appliquéd over freezer paper and removed the freezer paper when the blocks were finished.
- Appliqué A and B to C before positioning C on the background.
- Stitch down the shoe and add sole D last.

Sawtooth Border Assembly

- Piece a red triangle to a black triangle to create a square.
- Repeat so you have 112 pieced squares.
- Create border strips for the sides by piecing 2 strips of 30 pieced squares each. Note how Jean rotated the triangles in a different direction next to alternate blocks.
- Create similar strips for the top and bottom borders by piecing strips of 24 squares each.

Quilt Assembly

- Arrange the blocks, alternating colors and creating a general balance of left and right shoes.
- Stitch 5 rows of 4 blocks each.
- Attach the rows.
- Add the side sawtooth borders, then the top and bottom sawtooth borders.
- Add the narrow side strip borders, then the top and bottom narrow strips.
- Finish with the outer borders by adding the side borders, then the top and bottom.

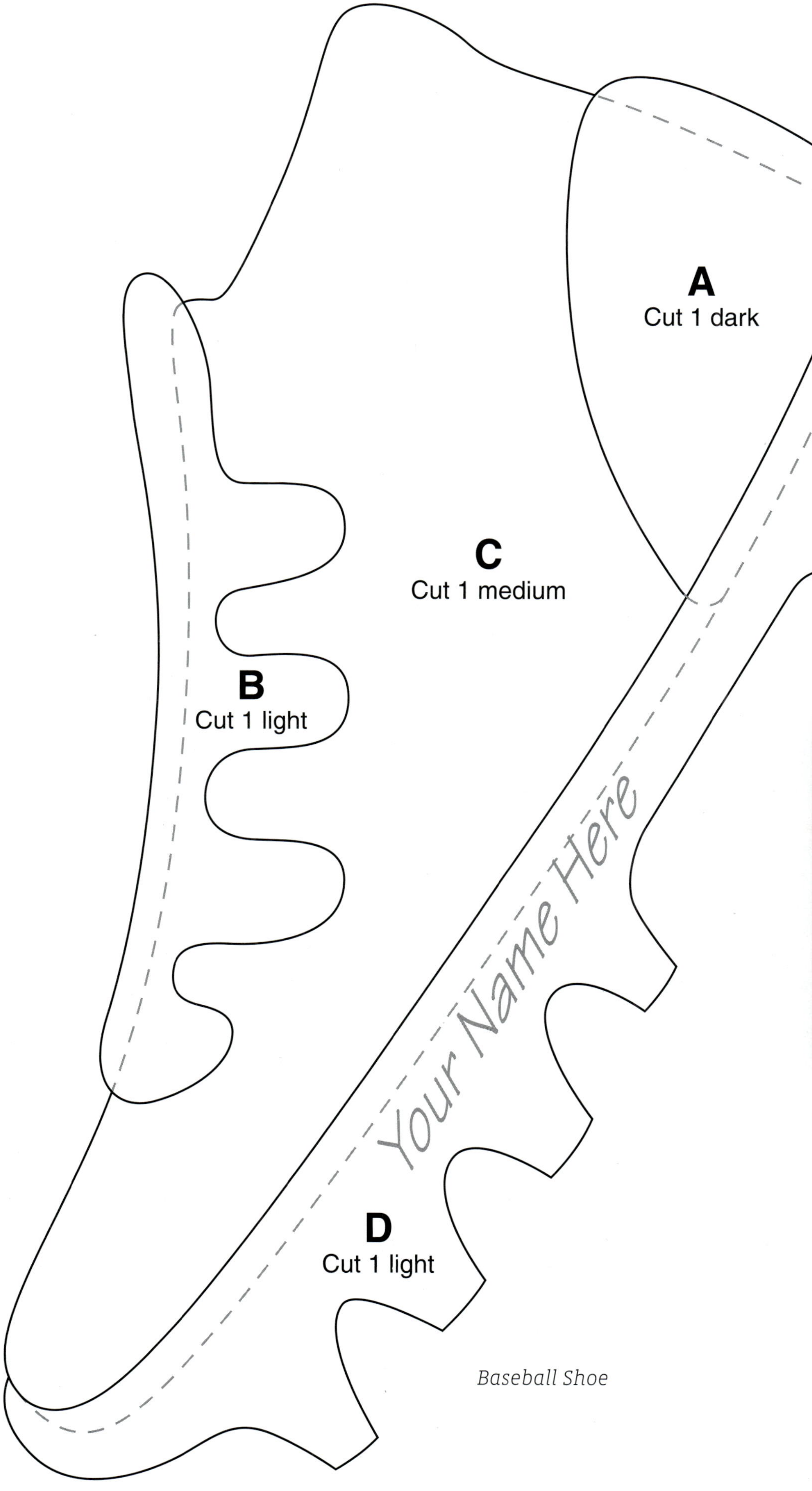

Baseball Shoe

Quilting

Because the quilt was dark, the quilting would not show up so Lori machine quilted it rather simply with meandering lines and outlines.

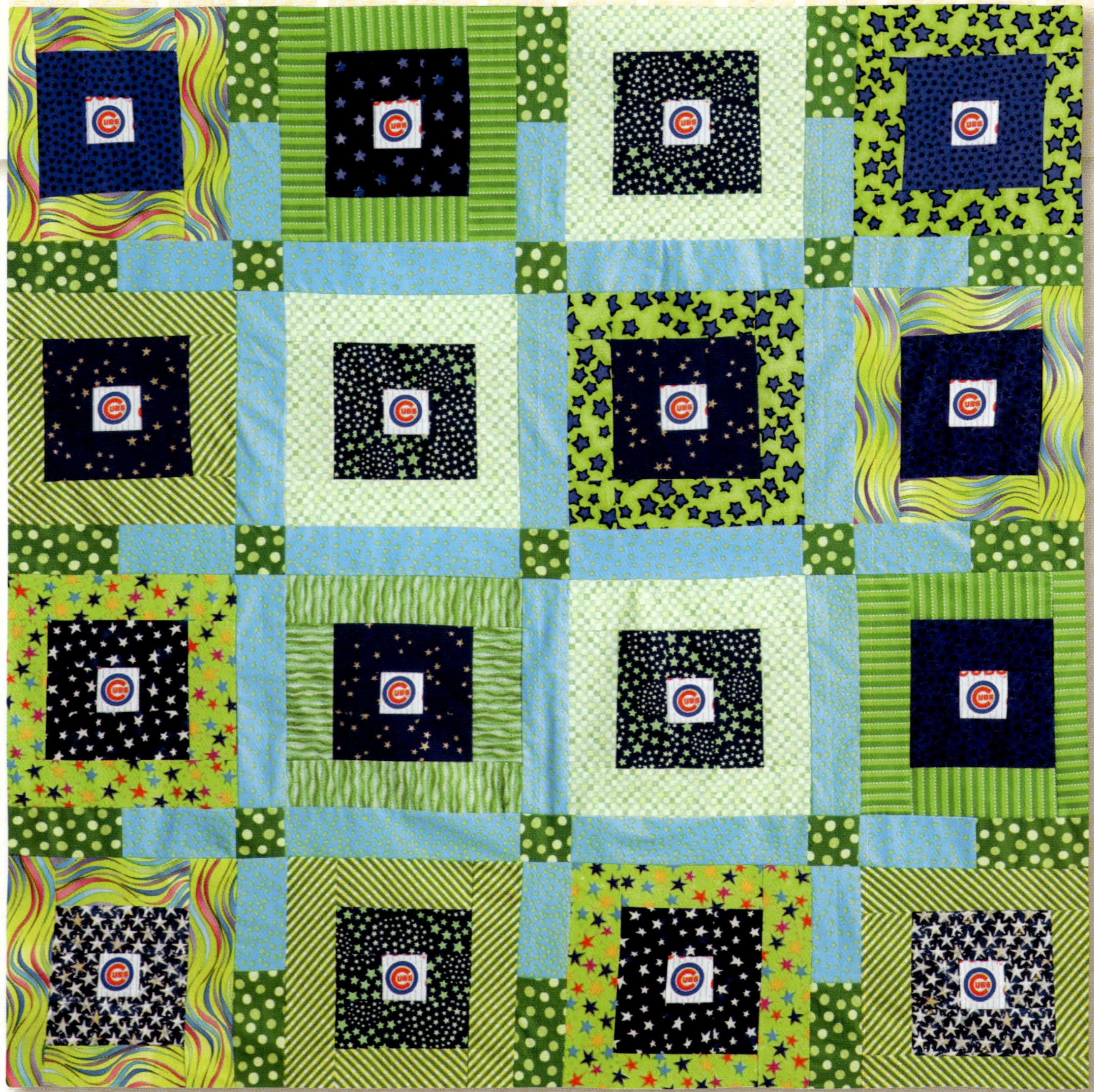

PROJECT 7

LOGS & LOGO QUILT

Logs & Logos by Barbara Brackman, 2010, Lawrence, Kansas, 46" x 46".

Baseball cards

Want to make a baby quilt for Cubs' fans - but they've chosen a lime-green and aqua color scheme for their future Ernie Banks's room? No problem, if you push the team color palette your way. Sky blue can symbolize all those sunny afternoon games; green the ivy-covered outfield wall. The housetops pattern can stand for prime real estate adjacent to Wrigley Field where fans watch games from the roofs of apartment buildings. The lesson here: Frame color symbolically and you can go anywhere.

Find a licensed team fabric and fussy-cut (isolate) the figures you like best. It's sometimes difficult to find the right team print - especially if you are a Padres fan who lives in Poughkeepsie. Use an internet search engine and type in the words Padres quilt fabric. I bet you'll find some.

Licensed fabrics have some legal restrictions. You are free to make as many quilts as you want to for your own use and for gifts, but selling quilts of team logos is not wise. If you want to make money selling Yankees or Steelers quilts, call the team and arrange to become a licensee.

Fabric Requirements

- Team logo fabric: 1/2 yard for center square (A) and backing. Be sure you can get 16 repeats.

Logs:

- Medium 1 1/2 yards
- Dark 3/4 yard

Sashing:

- Blue 1/2 yard
- Green 1/3 yard

Backing:

- 3 yards

Note: Decide how large your center square with its framed team logo is going to be before cutting these. If your square is going to be larger, buy extra fabric for the sashing.

Cutting Blocks

- Center squares (A): Fussy cut the team logo by centering it and deciding how much you want to include. I cut just the team symbol and left out the lettering. My square finished to 1 7/8". I added 1/2" for seam allowances and therefore my cut squares were 2 3/8". Cut 16.
- Logs: From the dark and medium fabrics, cut strips 2-1/2" x the width of fabric (wof).

Sashing

Decide how large your center square with its framed team logo is going to be before cutting these. If your square is going to be larger, cut sashing strips 1/2" longer than the finished block once you have finished a sample block.

Cut from the blues:

- H – 12 strips 2 1/2" x 10"
- F – 12 half strips 2 1/2" x 5 1/4"

Cut from the green:

- G – 9 squares 2 1/2" x 2 1/2"
- F – 12 half strips 2 1/2" x 5 1/4"

Block Assembly

Follow the block assembly instructions for Sew & Trim Log Cabin blocks on page 13. Your final trim size for step 14 will be 10" x 10". You need 16 blocks.

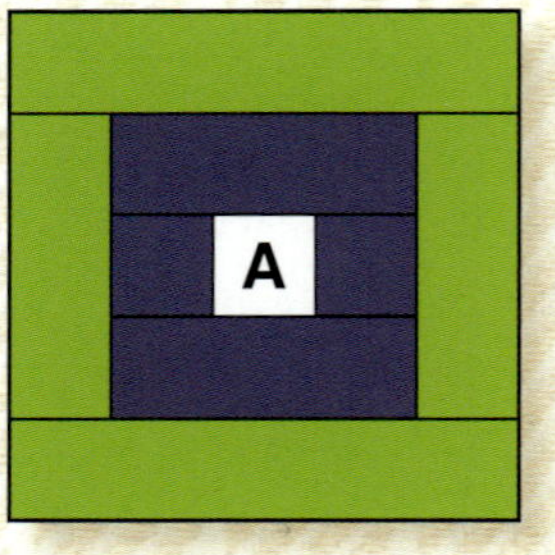

Quilt Assembly

- The split strips along the outside blocks are each pieced of a green and a blue rectangle (F). Piece 1 green F and 1 blue F end to end. Repeat to make 12 split strips. Press.
- For the top and bottom rows, stitch a split strip between each block as shown in the diagram. Make 2 rows of 4 blocks and 3 split strips. Place the green rectangles along the outside edge.
- Assemble the 2 center rows by piecing 3 blue strips (H) between 4 blocks as shown in the Assembly Diagram.
- Make a long sashing strip by piecing, beginning on the left, a split strip, a sashing square (G), and a blue strip (H). Continue piecing with a sashing square (G), blue strip (H), sashing square (G), and a split strip, making sure the green rectangle is at the end. Repeat to make 3 identical strips.
- Join rows together, alternating block rows with the long sashing strips.

Quilting

Quilting didn't get done for our deadline but we intend to play against the squares with circular lines and sunburst spikes centering on the logo.

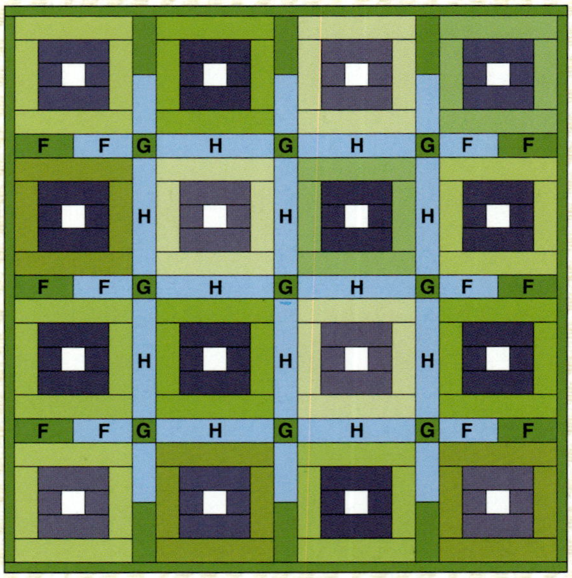

Assembly Diagram

PROJECT 8

LEBOWSKI FEST

Lebowski Fest by Jean Stanclift and Barbara Brackman. Quilted by Pamela Mayfield, 2006, Lawrence, Kansas, 46" x 46". Collection of Stacey Van Houten and Sheldon Weisgrau.

(left) My dad Ben Brackman about 1963.
(right) Pin boys in Burlington, Vermont, 1910. Photo by Lewis Hines, collection of the Library of Congress.

My neighbor Stacey and I collect bowling balls for yard ornaments (it's a good thing there are two of us to set neighborhood decorating standards). She asked me to create a bowling quilt for her husband, something they could show off at their Lebowski Fest parties. Jean Stanclift and I had a good time planning and sewing this ode to the alleys and a great movie. That purple border really pulls the quilt together.

Pin-ups in 1902. Bowlers keep score and grab attention with leg-revealing outfits.

Detail of an embroidered quilt top, about 1960, Mason City, Iowa. Collection of Ray Wilber and Cathy Dwigans. 38" x 57".
This quilt might have been made of old bowling shirts or may be a sampler of the kind of embroidery you could order for athletic apparel.

Fabric Requirements

Blocks

Note: fat quarters measure 18" x 22".

- Backgrounds: 4 pieces 3/4 yard each black prints (small colored spots on black add to the ambience)
- Balls: 9 fat quarters medium batiks or hand-dyed fabrics with swirls to imitate iridescent bowling balls
- Finger holes and shoe interiors: 1 fat quarter solid black
- Pins and shoe details: 1/2 yard white
- Pin decorations: 1 fat quarter red
- Shoes: 1 fat quarter each lime green and magenta

- Borders: 1 1/2 yards dark purple
- Backing: 2 3/4 yards
- Binding: extra 1/2 yard of the dark purple

Cutting

Blocks

Add a seam allowance to the appliqué templates and cut the pieces for the balls, shoes and pins from the templates on the following pages. We alternated 2 pin styles and reversed 2 shoes for lefts and rights.

Backgrounds

Ball and Shoe Blocks

- Cut 13 mixed black 8 1/2" squares.

Pin Blocks

- Cut 20 mixed black rectangles 8 1/2" x 5 3/4".

Borders

Inner Border

- Cut 2 purple strips 1 1/2" x 24 1/2" for side borders.
- Cut 2 purple strips 1 1/2" x 26 1/2" for top and bottom borders.

Outer Border

- Cut 2 purple strips 2 1/2" x 42 1/2" for side borders.
- Cut 2 purple strips 2 1/2" x 46 1/2" for top and bottom borders.

A retro bowling alley in Montrose, California, 2010.

Block Assembly

Appliqué the shoes using your favorite method. Jean machine-appliquéd over freezer paper and removed the freezer paper when the blocks were finished.

Pin boys in Lowell, Massachusetts in 1911 work at an establishment with the mysterious name of Les Miserables Bowling Alley. Is it a reference to the Alexander Dumas novel, a French-Canadian neighborhood or just a night of gutter balls? Photo by Lewis Hines, collection of the Library of Congress.

Balls

- Appliqué 3 finger holes (A) in a triangular configuration to the balls (B).
- Stitch the balls to the center of the background blocks. We moved the finger holes to different places in the blocks to create a balance. Make 9 blocks.

Pins

Pin #1

- Position and stitch 2 red stripes B to pin A, wrapping the raw edges under the pin.
- Position the pin in the center of the background 3/8" up from the seam line at the bottom.
- Appliqué the pin.
- You need 12 of pin #1.

Pin #2

- Position and stitch red crown (D) to pin A, tucking the raw edges behind the pin.
- Position the pin in the center of the background 3/8" up from the seam line at the bottom.
- Appliqué the pin.
- You need 8 of pin #2.

Shoes

- After basting or gluing the edges of shoe parts, layer the pieces to create a shoe before appliquéing it to the background.
- Begin with E and insert the sole C underneath. Baste or glue in place.
- Insert piece D so E remains on top. Baste or glue in place.
- Add piece B behind them so it looks like the inside of the shoe. Baste or glue in place.
- Position the 3 laces A last. Baste or glue in place.
- Center the shoe at an angle on the background and stitch.
- Repeat to make 4 shoes.

Bowlers in Bennington, Kansas about 1960.

Assembly Diagram

Quilt Assembly

- Make 3 rows of 3 balls, arranging the finger holes and colors for a balanced look.
- Add inner side border.
- Add inner top and bottom borders.
- Piece 5 pins together alternating pin #1 with #2 so you finish with pin #1 on each strip.
- Make 4 of these pin strips.
- Check to make sure your pin strips fit. If they are a bit longer than 26 1/2", they need to be trimmed 1/8" or so off each end.
- Piece a left and a right shoe to the top and bottom pin strips.
- Add the side pin borders.
- Add the top and bottom pin/shoe borders.
- Add the outer side borders.
- Add the outer top and bottom borders.

Quilting

Pam quilted a meandering line in the balls to emphasize the swirls. She echo-quilted the shapes in the pins and shoes to give them dimension and did more meandering lines in the background and border.

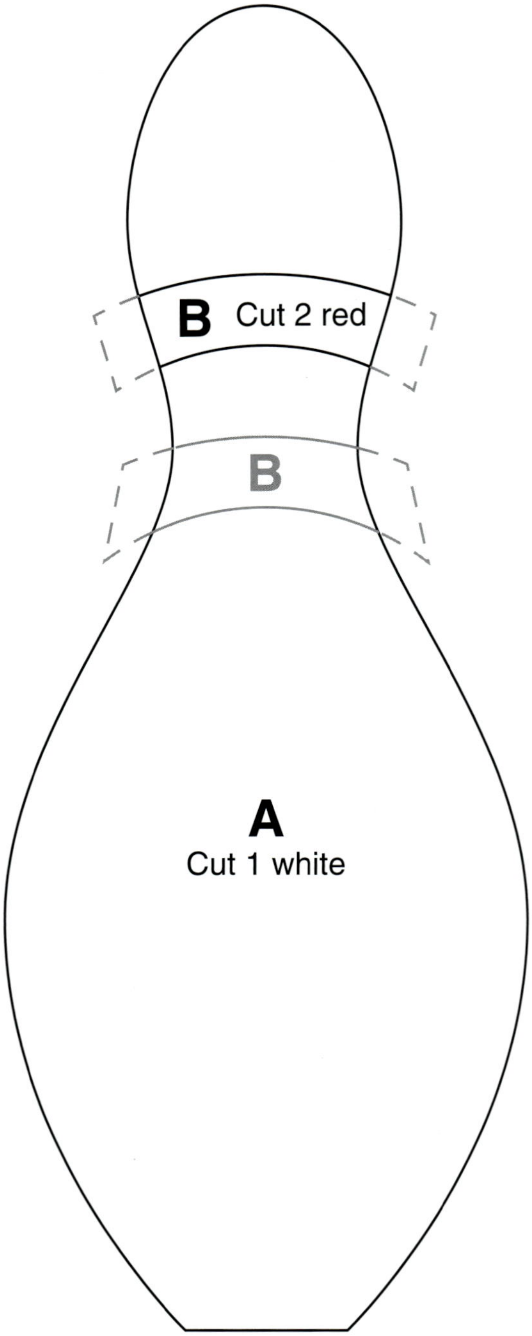
B Cut 2 red
B
A
Cut 1 white

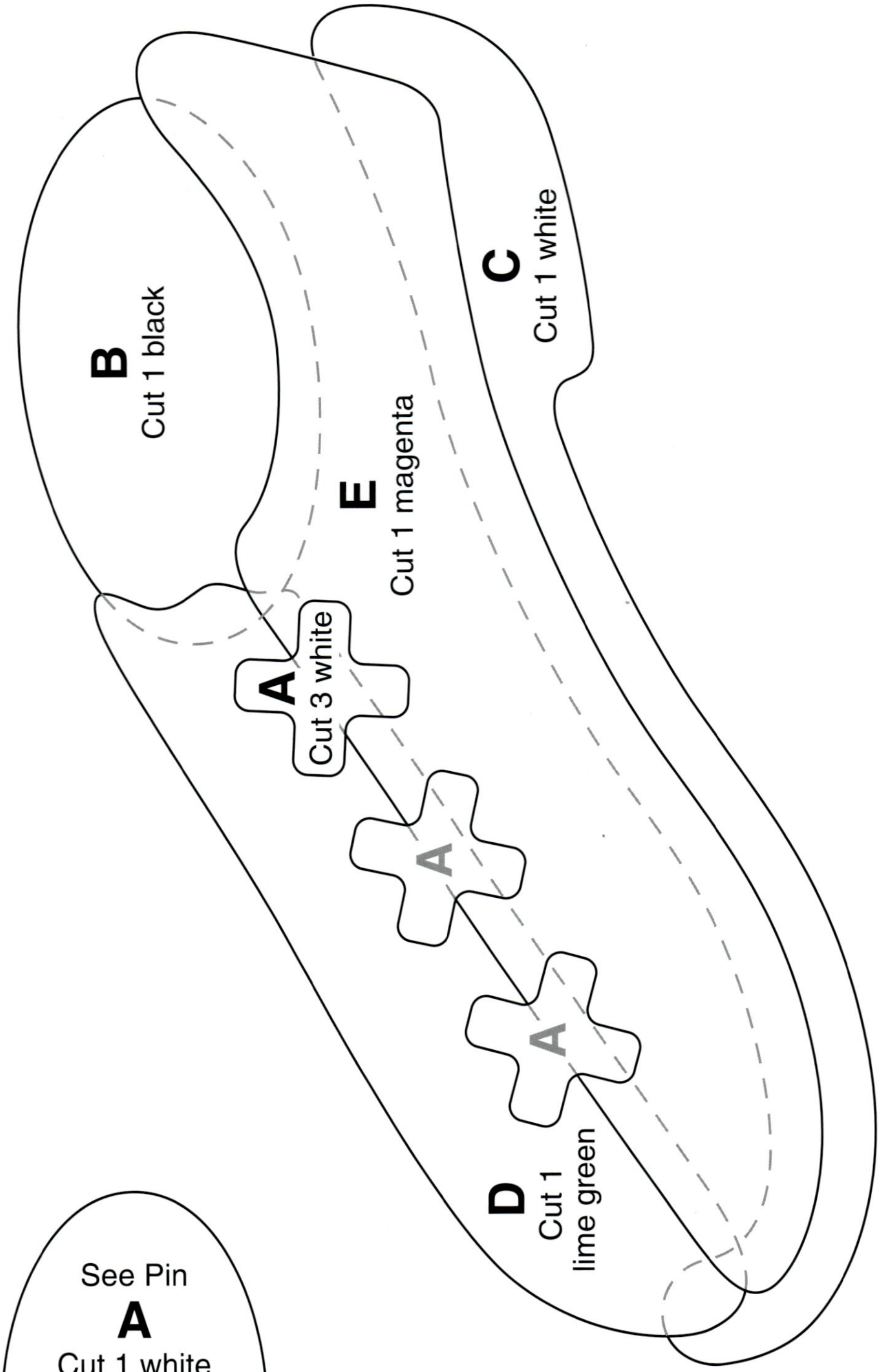
C
Cut 1 white
B
Cut 1 black
E
Cut 1 magenta
A
Cut 3 white
A
A
D
Cut 1
lime green

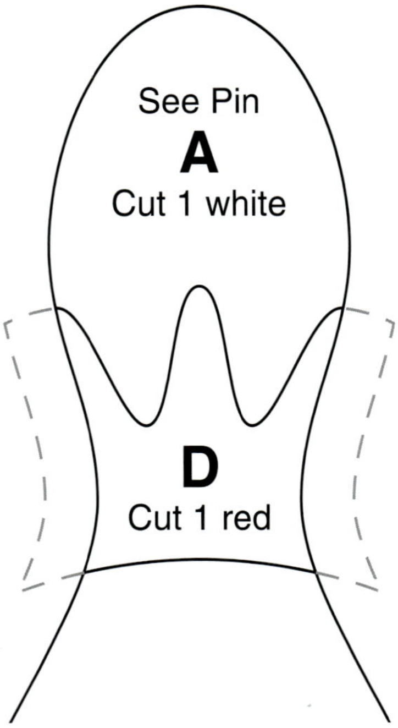
See Pin
A
Cut 1 white
D
Cut 1 red

A
Cut 3
black
3/4"
circles
B
Cut 1 swirly fabric

OTHER SHOES TO APPLIQUÉ

Template for running shoe

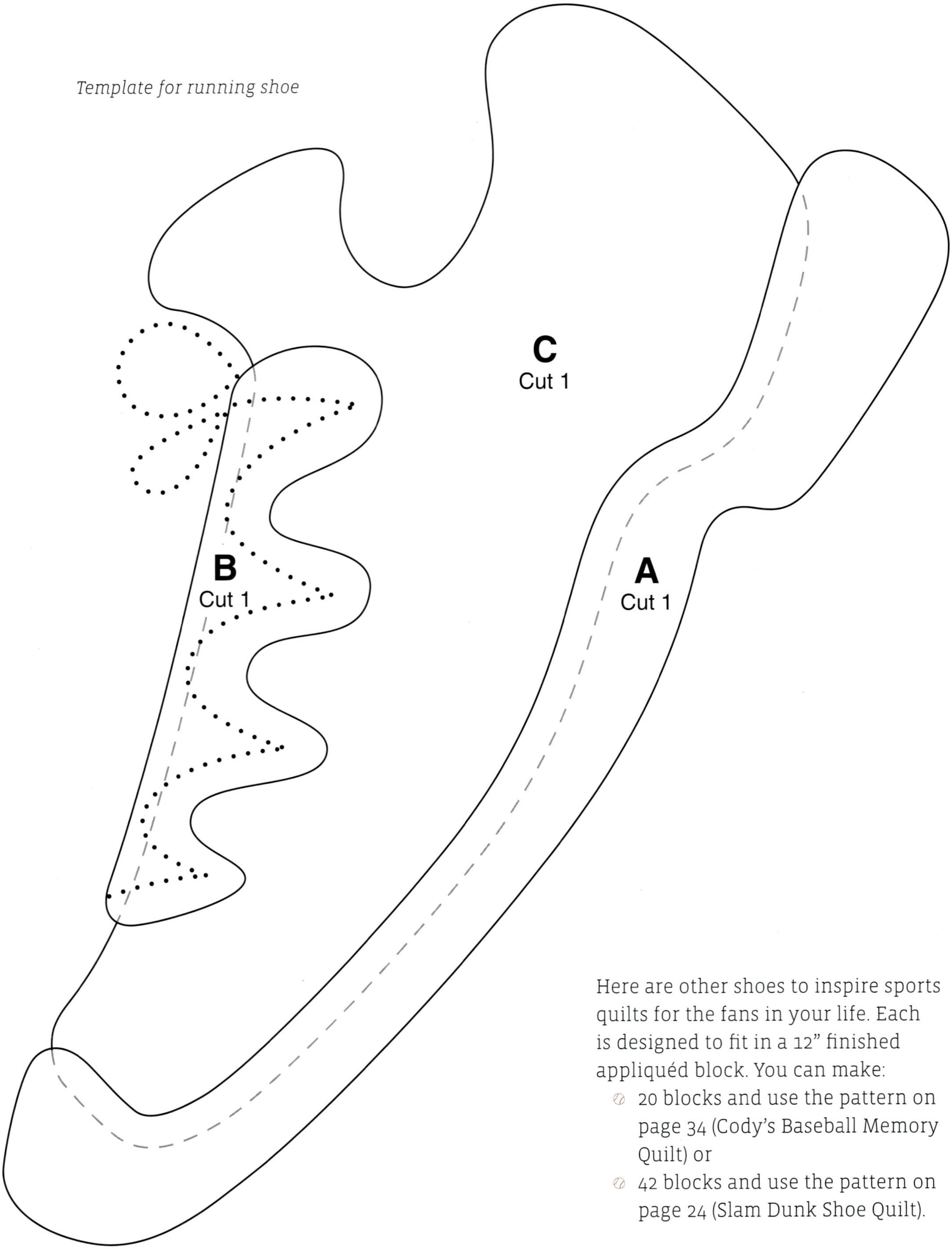

Here are other shoes to inspire sports quilts for the fans in your life. Each is designed to fit in a 12" finished appliquéd block. You can make:

- 20 blocks and use the pattern on page 34 (Cody's Baseball Memory Quilt) or
- 42 blocks and use the pattern on page 24 (Slam Dunk Shoe Quilt).

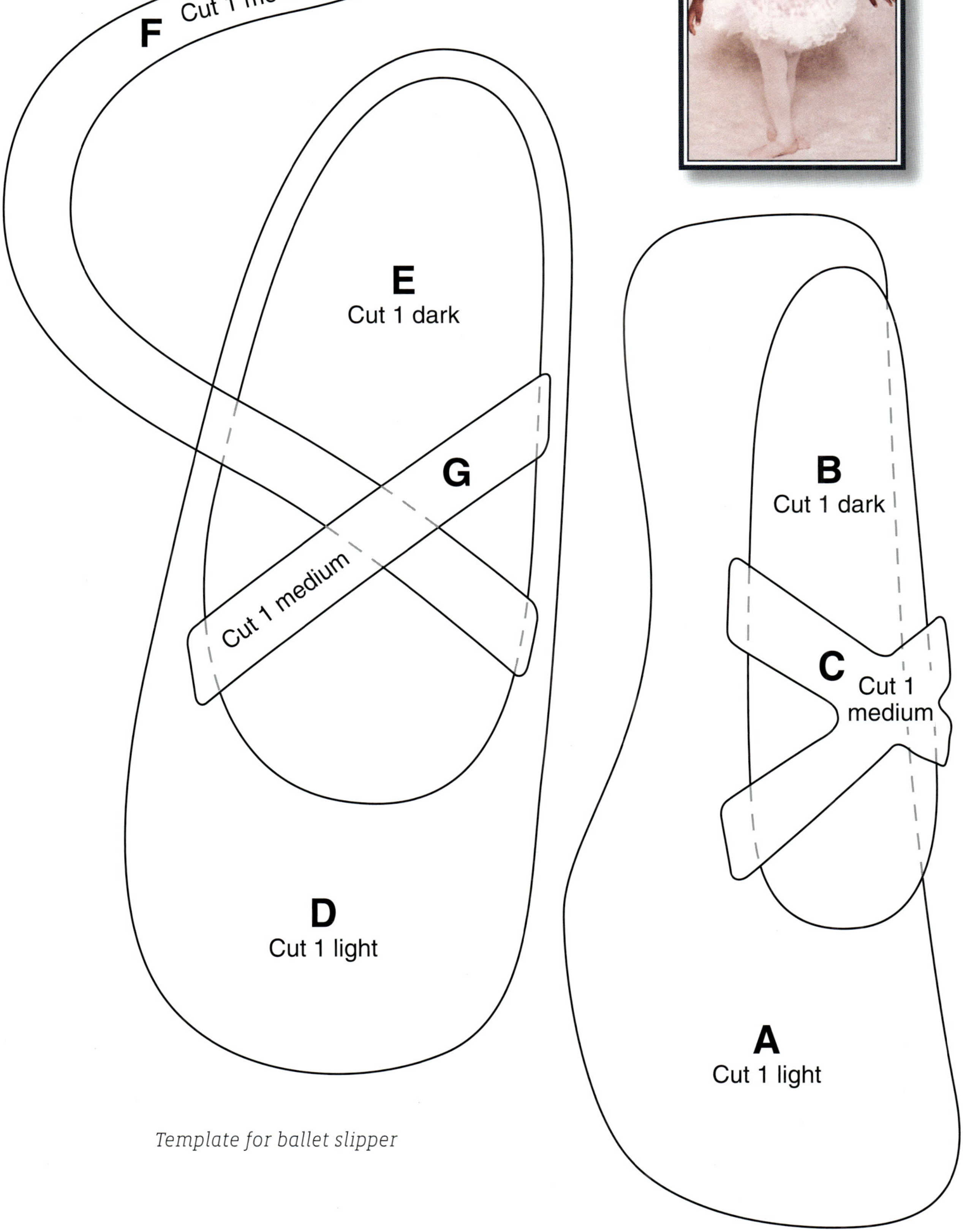

Template for ballet slipper

Template for roller skate

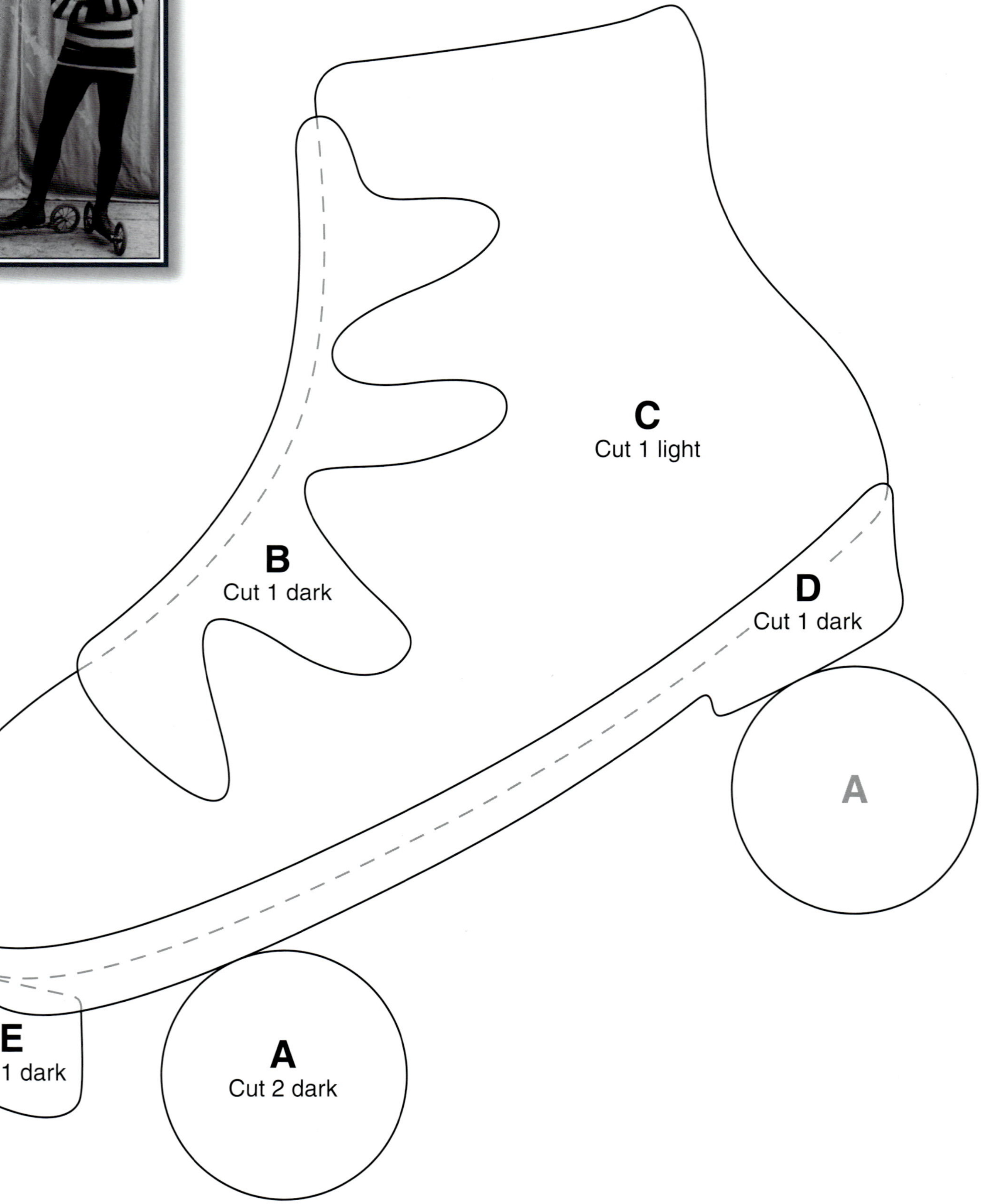

QUILTING DESIGNS

Quilters Lori Kukuk and Rosie Mayhew machine quilted sports imagery into the borders. Here are a few ideas.

Volleyball

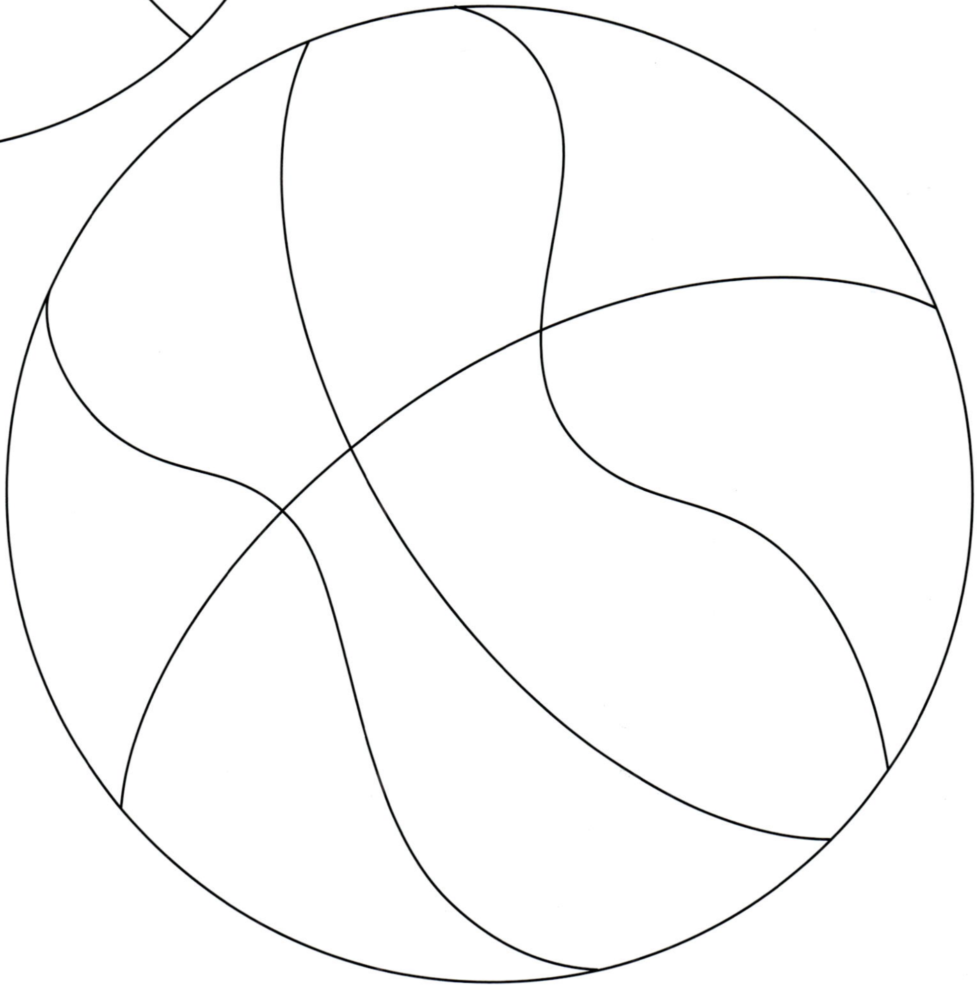

Basketball

Soccer

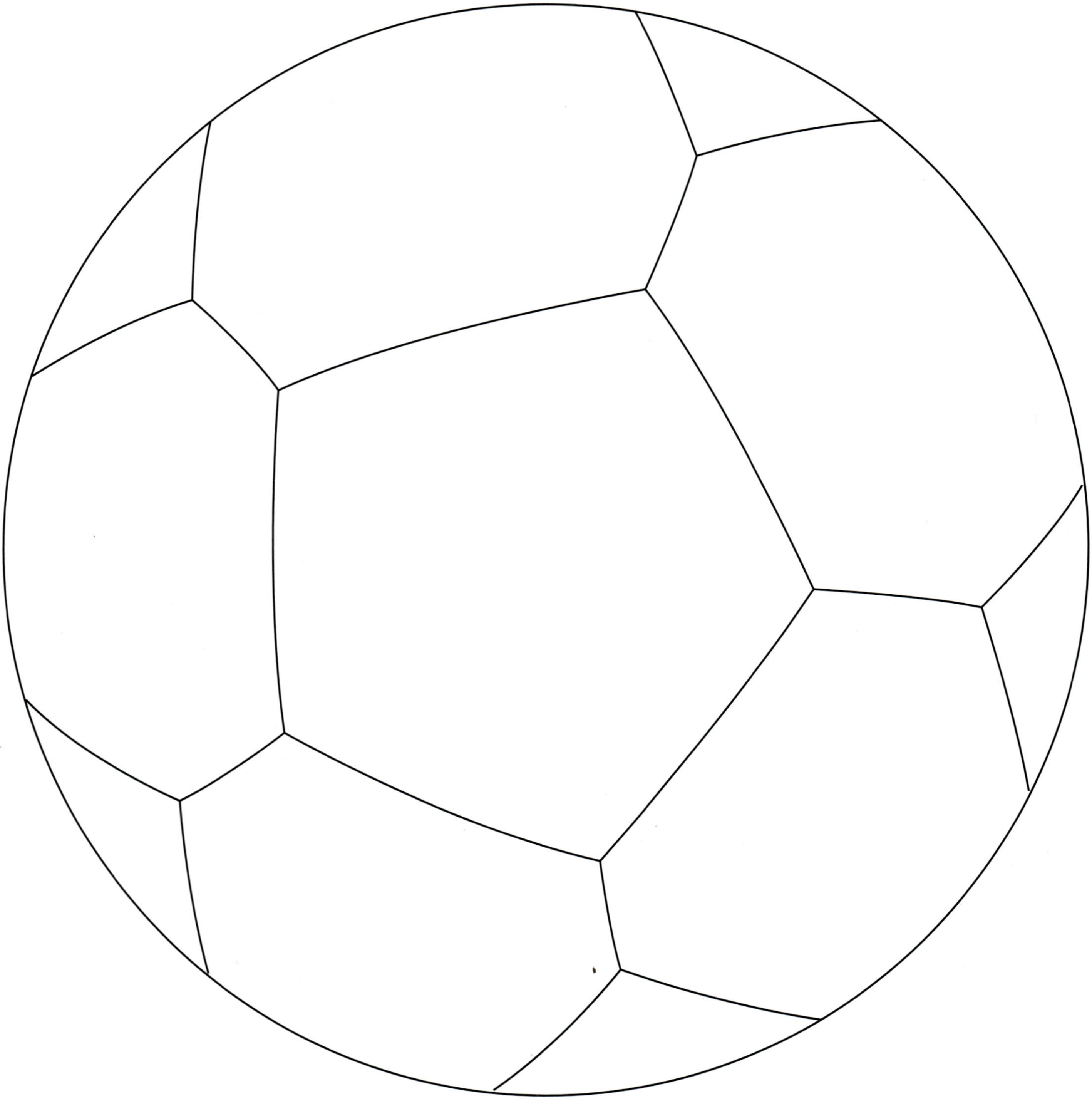

GALLERY

Prairie Fire, by Jean Stanclift, Lawrence, Kansas, 2002. Quilted by Lori Kukuk. 72" x 99". Jean adapted Baker University's team colors for this quilt for her son Michael. Rather than vivid orange and blue, she toned down the shades to an old-fashioned indigo blue and madder root orange. She found the pattern in an antique Amish quilt. It's a team quilt that is as welcome in Michael's grown-up decor as it was in his college dorm. Do notice the error in the pattern, which we didn't see until we photographed it. So much for the theory that quilters make deliberate mistakes. There are plenty of accidents.

Warm Up to the Home Team by Pamela Mayfield, Lawrence, Kansas, 2003. Pam made an all-team baseball quilt for Larry Mayfield using one of her favorite blocks, the traditional "Union Square." She created an all-over textured effect by combining team logo fabrics with baseball pictorials in the same general color family (a large family).

For Sydnei - Artiste & Athlete by Beverly Robinson and Lavon Broyles Wynn, Kansas City, Kansas, 2009. Quilted by Lynda Lyons. 70" x 82". Granny Beverly and neighbor Lavon made a quilt for Sydnei that captures memories from ballet to volleyball. They used a Sassy Pinwheels design from Kristin Gassaway to frame pictorial prints. See pictures of Sydnei on pages 16 and 49.

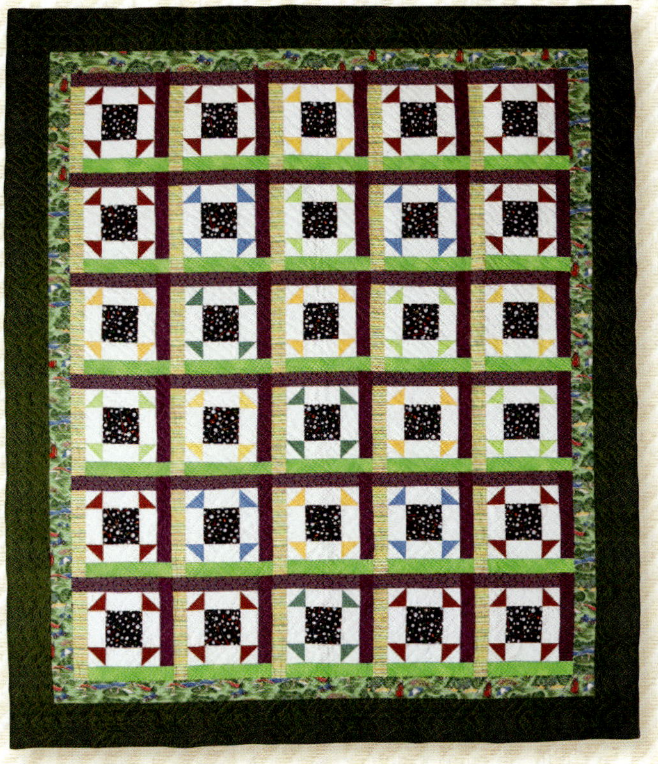

Hole in the Barn Door? No - Hole in One by Lavon Broyles Wynn, Kansas City, Kansas, 2009. Quilted by Lynda Lyons. 85" x 99". Neighbor Lavon Wynn found golf prints for a quilt for Gentry Gillespie and framed them with fabric featuring grass - Gentry always hits it right on the green.

Hockey Road by Mindy Peterson, 5acre Designs, Palmdale, California. 2003. 75" x 56". Mindy's husband Brian is a huge hockey fan so he got his very own hockey quilt for Christmas. The pattern is Yellow Brick Road by Atkinson Designs.

What's in My Pockets by Barbara Gerdes Fife, Overland Park, Kansas, 2009. 52" x 52". Grandma made a quilt with 3-D pockets, based on Tracey Brookshier's Party Bags pattern, for Liam Fife's sister. Liam, an all-round athlete, hinted he'd like one for his tenth birthday---but no floral prints. His grandmother chose a variety of sports fabric and was sure to include a golf print as that's his favorite. He can keep sports memorabilia in the appropriate pockets.

Stay Connected by Gloria A. Clark, Kansas City, Kansas, 2009. 65" x 54". Gloria A. Clark has a family of Super Stars (see daughter Gloria E. and son Kelvin on page 25) so she found sports prints to represent each of their interests. Her husband, two sons and daughter love this "All-Sports Quilt" because it reminds them of their individual achievements and family connections.